My Body

My Heart and Lungs

Sally Hewitt

QEB Publishing

Library of Congress Control Number:
2008011712

ISBN 978 1 59566 554 6

Printed and bound in China

Author Sally Hewitt

Consultant Terry Jennings
Project Editor Judith Millidge
Designer Kim Hall
Picture Researcher Claudia Tate
Illustrator Chris Davidson

Publisher Steve Evans
Creative Director Zeta Davies

Picture credits

Key: t = top, b = bottom, m = middle,
l =left, r = right

Alamy Bubbles Photolibrary 11
Corbis Daniel Attia /Zefa 14, Jim Craigmyle 18
Getty Images Mel Yates 6, Stephen Frink 13, Kevin
Mackintosh 16
Science Photo Library Mauro Fermariello 10
Shutterstock Wizdata inc 4, Z Adam 4l, Jaimie Duplass
5b, Gelpi 5t, Supri Suharjoto 8, Darren Baker 9,
Juriah Mosim 15, Arvind Balarama 17b, Julian Rovagnati 17t,
Thomas M Perkins 19t, Vadim Ponomarenko 19b,
Olga Lyubkina 20r, StudioNewmarket 20l, Yvan Dube 21b,
Hallgerd 21t

**Words in bold are
explained in the glossary
on page 22.**

Contents

What is your heart?

Your heart is a strong **muscle** about the size of your fist. It has two pumps that push your **blood** around your body. Your heart sits just to the left of the middle of your chest.

Heart shapes are everywhere, on balloons, cards, and cuddly toys. But your real heart looks quite different.

4

Your heart never stops working. It **pumps** your blood all day and all night to every part of your body. Your brain, lungs, skin, and muscles need blood to keep them working properly.

A doctor uses a stethoscope to listen to your heart pumping in your chest.

Your heart doesn't work as hard when you are asleep. When you wake up and start moving it beats faster.

Heart beat

Your heart is hollow, which means it has empty space inside it. The space fills up with blood, then your heart muscles squeeze and push the blood out again.

Your heart beats every time your heart muscles squeeze tight.

Activity

Fill a balloon with water. Your heart fills up with blood like this. Gently squeeze the balloon with your hand. This is like your heart muscles squeezing. Watch the water squirt out. Blood spurts out of your heart and into your blood vessels in the same way.

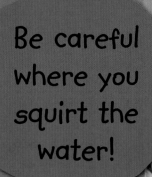

Be careful where you squirt the water!

6

There are two sides of your heart, the left side and the right side. Each side has two rooms or chambers. The right side of your heart pumps blood into your lungs to collect **oxygen**. The left side of your heart pumps blood into your body.

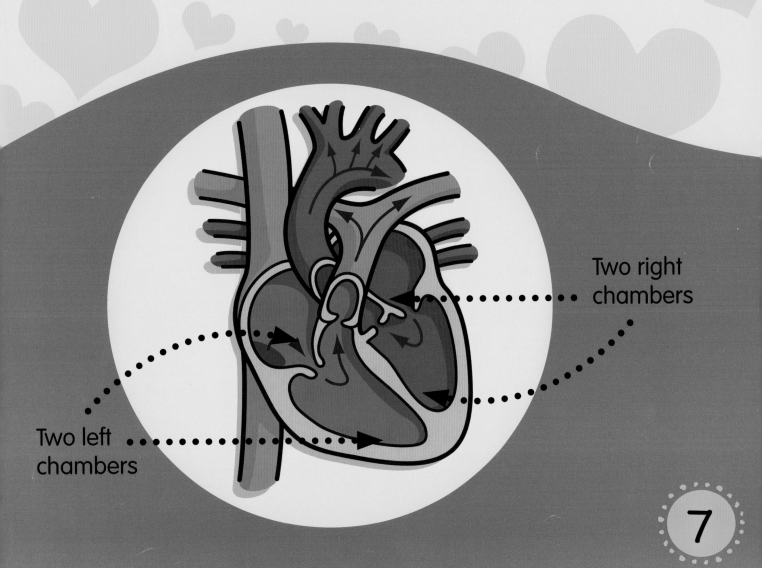

Two right chambers

Two left chambers

Veins and arteries

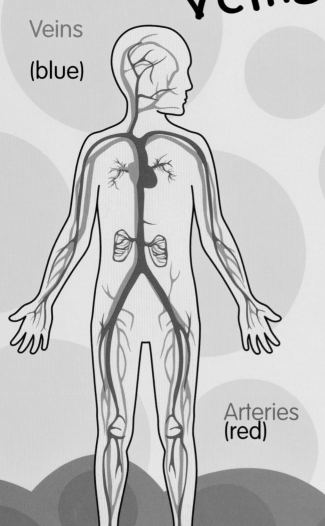

Your heart pumps your blood into tubes called **blood vessels**. Blood vessels called arteries carry blood away from your heart to every other part of your body. Blood vessels called veins bring blood back to your heart.

When you exercise, your body warms up and sometimes your skin turns red. This is because blood rushes to the blood vessels in your skin to keep you cool.

8

Around and around

Your blood is always moving around your body and through your heart. This movement is called circulation. It takes less than a minute for your heart to pump blood to every part of your body!

Activity

You can *see* blood flowing through your hand. Hold your right hand in the air for a few moments. Hang your left hand down by your side. Now look at the color of each hand. It is harder for your heart to pump blood upward, so your right hand looks pale because there is less blood in it. It is easy for blood to flow downward, so your left hand is red because it is full of blood.

9

Blood

Your blood is like a delivery truck. It carries oxygen from your lungs and goodness from your food to every part of your body.

Your blood is full of tiny cells, which carry the oxygen. These cells give your blood its red color.

If you fall and cut yourself, your blood dries into a hard scab and your skin heals underneath the scab.

Feel the beat

When you are working hard, if you are running for example, your body needs more oxygen from your blood, so your heart beats faster.

You can feel your heart beat in the blood vessels on your wrists. This is called your pulse.

Activity

Feel your pulse. Now run on the spot for a few moments. Feel your pulse again.

Your heart usually beats about 90 times a minute.

Your pulse gets faster when you work hard.

Lungs

Nose

Mouth

Windpipe

Ribs

Lungs

Your lungs are the part of your body you **breathe** with. They are like two big sacks in your chest. Your left lung is a bit smaller than your right lung to make room for your heart. Your lungs are protected by your ribs.

The insides of your lungs are like sponges. They soak up air instead of water.

Ribs

Lung muscle that squeezes air in and out.

Spongy inside of lung.

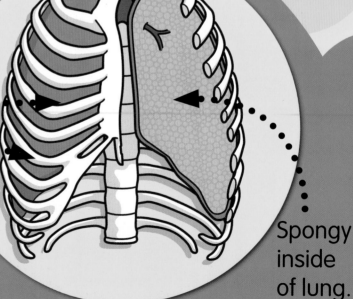

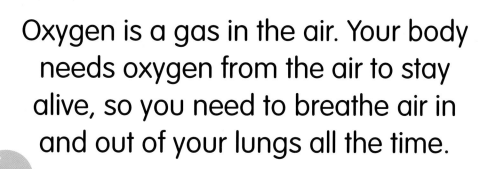

Oxygen is a gas in the air. Your body needs oxygen from the air to stay alive, so you need to breathe air in and out of your lungs all the time.

Humans can't breathe under water, unless they use a tube called a snorkel while swimming.

Breathing in

You breathe air in through your mouth and nose. Air goes down your **windpipe** into your lungs. As your lungs fill up, they get bigger.

Tiny hairs in your nose and windpipe catch bits of dirt and help to clean the air going into your lungs.

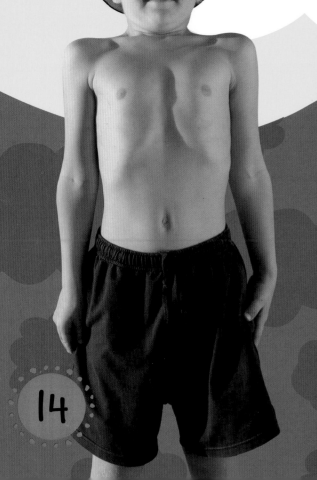

Activity

You can feel your lungs fill with air. Put your hands on your ribs. Breathe in deeply. Feel your ribs lift and your chest get bigger as your lungs fill with air.

Oxygen from the air goes into tiny blood vessels called capillaries in your lungs. Blood full of oxygen flows to your heart and your heart pumps it all around your body.

When you work hard, your heart and lungs work hard, too, and give you the extra oxygen that your body needs.

Breathing out

When you breathe in, fresh air goes into your lungs. After your lungs have taken oxygen from the air, you breathe it out. The stale air goes up your windpipe and out through your mouth and nose.

The air you breathe out gets warm as it goes through your body.

Activity

Put your hand near your mouth and breathe on it. Your breath feels warm.

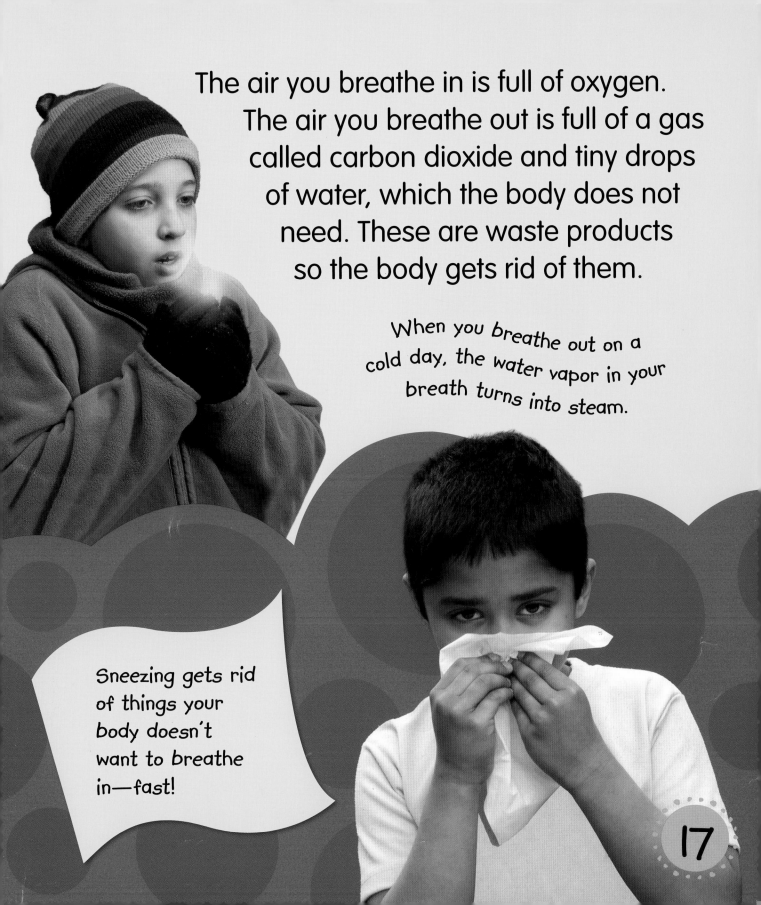

The air you breathe in is full of oxygen. The air you breathe out is full of a gas called carbon dioxide and tiny drops of water, which the body does not need. These are waste products so the body gets rid of them.

When you breathe out on a cold day, the water vapor in your breath turns into steam.

Sneezing gets rid of things your body doesn't want to breathe in—fast!

17

Blah Blah Blah Blah Blah

Talking

You need your lungs to breathe and to talk. You speak and sing with the small lump you can see and feel in your throat called your voice box, or larynx.

Activity

Feel your voice box. Make all kinds of different sounds—shout, screech, and whisper. Does your voice box move when you make a sound?

18

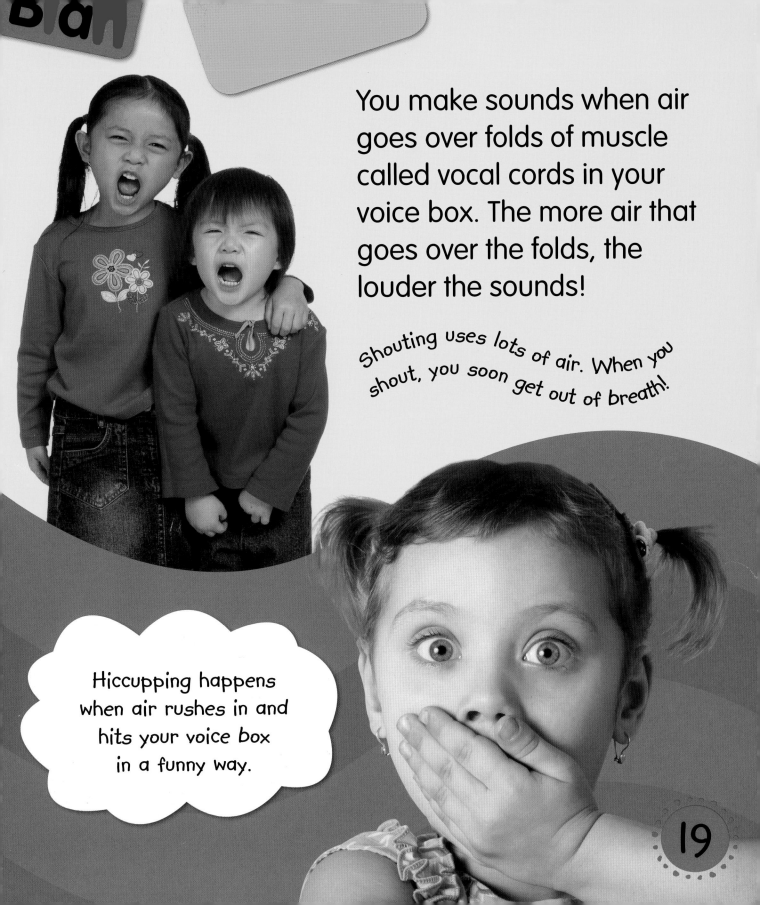

You make sounds when air goes over folds of muscle called vocal cords in your voice box. The more air that goes over the folds, the louder the sounds!

Shouting uses lots of air. When you shout, you soon get out of breath!

Hiccupping happens when air rushes in and hits your voice box in a funny way.

Healthy heart and lungs

Look after your heart and lungs. Keeping active makes your heart and lungs work harder. Hard work makes them strong and healthy so they can help to keep your whole body healthy.

Healthy eating

You can help protect your heart, blood vessels, and lungs by eating fresh food, lots of fruit and vegetables, and not too much fat, salt, or sugar.

Healthy food is good for you and delicious, too!

Fresh air

Fresh air is good for your lungs. Sometimes the air in big cities is polluted by fumes from cars. Polluted air is bad for you because it contains tiny bits of smoke and dust that enter your lungs and make you cough.

Take a trip to the countryside or to the seaside where the air is fresh and clean.

Sleep

When you are asleep your brain makes sure you keep breathing in and out during the night without having to think about it.

When you wake up after a good night's sleep, you are rested and ready for a busy day.

21

Glossary

Blood
Blood is the red liquid that runs through your blood vessels to every part of your body. It carries goodness from your food and oxygen from your lungs.

Blood vessels
Blood vessels are tubes that carry your blood. Arteries are blood vessels that carry blood away from your heart. Veins are blood vessels that carry blood back to your heart.

Breathe
You breathe air in and out of your lungs all the time. You breathe through your nose and mouth.

Muscles
Your muscles pull your bones so you can move. Muscles keep your heart beating and your lungs breathing.

Oxygen
Oxygen is a gas in the air. Your lungs take oxygen from the air when you breathe in. Your blood carries oxygen from your lungs around your body.

Pump
A pump pushes liquid along. Your heart is a pump that pushes blood through your blood vessels.

Windpipe
Your windpipe is the tube that carries air into your lungs when you breathe in, and carries it out again when you breathe out.

Notes for parents and teachers

1. Point to the position of your heart, just to the left and middle of your chest. Make a fist to show the size of your heart. An adult's fist is bigger than a child's fist. Talk about the comparative size of a child's heart and an adult's heart.

2. Feel your ribs and breastbone. Discuss how your ribs protect your heart. Explain that your heart needs to be protected because it is soft. Use the word "muscle" and feel other muscles that let you move. Use the word "pump" and talk about how a pump pushes liquid.

3. Talk about how blood travels through blood vessels in the same way that water travels through pipes. Find pipes around the home. Talk about what happens to water without pipes to travel through!

4. Find the blood vessels in your wrist. Feel each other's pulse and explain that each beat is your heart pumping blood all around your body.

5. Breathe in and out through your nose and mouth. Try putting your hand in front of your face. Feel air coming out of your nose. Now feel it coming out of your mouth. Does air come out of both your nose and your mouth at the same time?

6. Run together on the spot and feel how your heart beats faster and you breathe more quickly after exercise. Explain that this is because your body needs more oxygen when you work hard. Feel your heart beat and notice that your breathing slows down when you rest.

Index